Deadly Disasters

World's Worst VOLCANIC ERUPTIONS

Janey Levy

PowerKiDS press
New York

Published in 2009 by The Rosen Publishing Group, Inc.
29 East 21st Street, New York, NY 10010

First Edition

Editor: Nicole Pristash
Book Design: Greg Tucker
Photo Researcher: Jessica Gerweck

Photo Credits: Cover © Richard A. Cook III/Getty Images; p. 5 © AFP/Getty Images; p. 7 Shutterstock.com; pp. 9, 10–11 by Digital Vision; p. 13 © Pacific Stock/SuperStock; p. 15 © NASA/Science Source; p. 17 © age fotostock/SuperStock; p. 19 © Jacques Langevin/CORBIS SYGMA; p. 21 © G. Brad Lewis/Getty Images.

Library of Congress Cataloging-in-Publication Data

Levy, Janey.
  World's worst volcanic eruptions / Janey Levy.
      p. cm. — (Deadly disasters)
  Includes index.
  ISBN 978-1-4042-4512-9 (library binding) ISBN 978-1-4042-4536-5 (pbk)
ISBN 978-1-4042-4554-9 (6-pack)
  1. Volcanoes—Juvenile literature. I. Title.
  QE521.3.L48 2009
  551.21—dc22
                                                2008007750

Manufactured in the United States of America

Contents

Volcanic Eruptions

A volcano is an opening in Earth's **surface** through which hot, melted rock **erupts**. Volcanoes are found around the world. Some are **active**, which means they still erupt. Others are inactive, which means they have not erupted in a very long time.

Volcanic eruptions can be deadly. When they erupt, volcanoes send **ash** and dust into the air. **Lava** flows burn and destroy homes and crops. The worst eruption in history happened in Indonesia in 1815. The Tambora volcano erupted and killed around 92,000 people. Volcanic eruptions have happened often, but some throughout history have been terrible and very deadly.

Some volcanoes erupt a large cloud of ash and steam, called a plume. Ash plumes can rise many miles (km) into the air, like this volcano plume on Réunion, a French island in the Indian Ocean.

Volcanoes Around the World

Most volcanoes are found in a band around the Pacific Ocean, called the Ring of Fire. Volcanoes are also found in other parts of the world, such as Hawaii, Iceland, Africa, and Europe. Some volcanoes are even found on the ocean bottom!

Volcanoes are sorted into groups based on their shape and what they are made of. **Shield** volcanoes are low and wide. They are made of lava. **Cinder** cones are shaped like cones and are made of **tephra**. Stratovolcanoes are also cone shaped. They are made of lava and tephra. Stratovolcanoes are also called **composite** volcanoes.

This is a stratovolcano in eastern Russia, called Klyuchevskaya Sopka. Klyuchevskaya is one of the most active volcanoes in the North Pacific Ocean. It erupts about once every two years.

How a Volcano Forms

A volcano begins as magma, or hot and melted rock, deep inside Earth. Gas mixed with the magma makes the magma lighter than the rock around it. The magma then rises toward Earth's surface. It melts the rock around it and forms a large space, called a magma **chamber**.

The weight of the rock around the chamber presses on the magma and causes the magma to rise. The magma and gas melt a path to the surface and blast through it. This blast forms an opening, called a vent. Magma turns to lava when it comes out of the vent. The eruption has begun!

Lava can destroy everything in its path, such as this road.

Pages 10–11: This is a lava fountain, which is made when lava sprays up from a volcanic crack or hole.

10

11

During and After an Eruption

Eruptions have different amounts of power. Sometimes lava flows quietly and sometimes it blasts high into the air. Other eruptions blast out tephra and send gases and cinders several miles (km) up. The most powerful eruptions send clouds of hot gases, ash, dust, and tephra rushing down the volcano and may blow the volcano apart.

Hot lava destroys everything it touches. Eruptions can cause **landslides** and **mudflows** that destroy towns and kill people. So much ash can fall that towns are completely covered. Dust in the air can keep out sunlight and change the weather for years. Many eruptions like this have happened throughout history.

This is the crater of the Kilauea volcano in Hawaii. A circular crater is made around the vent when steam, ash, and lava erupt from the vent.

The Biggest Eruption in History

The biggest eruption ever recorded was of Tambora, in the Southeast Asian country of Indonesia, in 1815. Tambora sent out huge amounts of gas, ash, and a type of tephra called pumice. Ash fell 4 inches (10 cm) deep in some places. Roofs fell from the weight of the ash, and crops died. Up to 92,000 people were killed from the eruption and from the hunger and sickness that followed.

The dust and ash in the air from the eruption blocked the sunlight and made all of Earth colder for years. People called 1816 the year without a summer because it was so cold.

This picture of Tambora's caldera was taken from the spacecraft *Discovery*. A caldera forms following an eruption, when land above the magma chamber caves in after the chamber empties.

15

Krakatau

Krakatau is another volcano that had one of the world's worst eruptions. Krakatau is an island in Indonesia. There was no one living on Krakatau when it erupted in 1883. However, the eruption killed thousands of people.

People as far as 3,000 miles (4,828 km) away from Krakatau heard the powerful eruption. It sent out huge amounts of dust, ash, and pumice, which destroyed most of the island. The eruption also caused tsunamis, which are giant ocean waves. Some waves were more than 100 feet (30 m) high. More than 36,000 people died when Krakatau erupted. Most of these deaths were caused by the tsunamis.

Today, Krakatau is still an active volcano. It has erupted many times since 1883. These later eruptions, like the one shown here, were much smaller than the 1883 eruption.

Nevado del Ruiz

Nevado del Ruiz is a volcano in Colombia, in South America. In 1985, it had a terrible eruption that killed many people.

An ice cap covers Nevado del Ruiz's top. However, ash, pumice, and lava melted part of the ice cap when the volcano erupted. Water from the melted ice cap caused mudflows, which raced down the volcano. One mudflow was about 100 feet (30 m) high. It was filled with huge rocks that destroyed a dam and started a flood. The flood and mud hit the town of Armero and destroyed it. About 23,000 people and 15,000 animals were killed.

This is the town of Armero, Colombia, after the eruption of Nevado del Ruiz. Rock and water flowed down the volcano, and totally flooded the town.

Keeping Safe from Volcanic Eruptions

Scientists study a volcano's changes along with its past eruptions to learn how a volcano acts. They use special tools to study activity in the volcano. This helps scientists know whether an eruption is coming. Scientists will tell government leaders if they believe a volcano will erupt. People on TV and the radio will then tell everyone what is happening and to leave home if it is necessary.

Volcanoes will always erupt. History has proven that volcanoes can be deadly. However, staying away from a volcano during an eruption is the best way to keep yourself safe from harm.

This scientist is studying volcanic eruptions by taking small samples, or pieces, of lava from a volcano in Hawaii. The samples will help him learn more about eruptions.

Volcanic Eruption Facts

Laki, in Iceland, erupted in 1783. Harmful gases killed more than 10,000 cows, 27,000 horses, and 190,000 sheep. More than 10,000 people died from hunger.

Mount Pelée, in the West Indies, erupted in 1902. Only several people from the town of St. Pierre lived through the eruption. About 30,000 people died altogether.

Vesuvius, in Italy, is famous for its many eruptions. One eruption completely destroyed the city of Pompeii in the year 79.

Mount St. Helens, in the state of Washington, erupted in 1980. The force knocked down a lot of trees. It destroyed buildings, roads, and bridges. Fifty-seven people died.

Glossary

active *(AK-tiv)* Busy or doing something.

ash *(ASH)* Pieces of tiny rock that shoot out of a volcano when it erupts.

chamber *(CHAYM-bur)* A closed space.

cinder *(SIN-der)* A small piece of burned wood.

composite *(kom-PAH-zut)* Made of more than one kind of matter.

erupts *(ih-RUPTS)* Breaks through.

landslides *(LAND-slydz)* Movements of rock or earth down a hill.

lava *(LAH-vuh)* Hot, melted rock.

mudflows *(MUD-flohz)* Mud that flows at high speed down the sides of a volcano.

scientists *(SY-un-tists)* People who study the world.

shield *(SHEELD)* Like a large, slightly rounded disk carried by fighters to keep them safe during battle.

surface *(SER-fes)* The outside of anything.

tephra *(TEH-fruh)* Hard matter erupted from a volcano.

Index

A
ash, 4, 12, 14, 16, 18

C
crops, 4, 14

D
dust, 4, 12, 14, 16

H
history, 4, 12, 20
home(s), 4, 20

I
Iceland, 6, 22

Indonesia, 4, 14, 16

L
lava flows, 4

M
mudflow(s), 12, 18

O
ocean bottom, 6

P
Pacific Ocean, 6
people, 4, 12, 14, 16, 18, 20, 22

R
Ring of Fire, 6
rock(s), 4, 8, 18

S
scientists, 20
shape, 6
shield volcanoes, 6
stratovolcanoes, 6
surface, 4, 8

T
Tambora, 4, 14
tephra, 6, 12, 14

Web Sites

Due to the changing nature of Internet links, PowerKids Press has developed an online list of Web sites related to the subject of this book. This site is updated regularly. Please use this link to access the list:

www.powerkidslinks.com/disast/volcanic/